Twenty-One Memories

Sam Verge

BookLeaf
Publishing

India | USA | UK

Presentation by *BookLeaf Publishing*

Web: www.bookleafpub.com

E-mail: info@bookleafpub.com

ISBN: 978-93-5744-920-5

First edition 2022

ACKNOWLEDGEMENT

I would like to acknowledge my wonderful partner for standing by me through all of these moments, good and bad.

How to be Perfect

Don't talk
Don't think
Don't yell
Don't cry
Don't be rude
Don't quarrel

Anything but happiness isn't perfection

Take notes
Do the homework
Perfect the homework
Take tests
Pass the tests
Not good enough.

Anything but A's isn't perfection

Listen
Smile
Obey
Your opinions don't matter
Frustration and anger is for adults
Suppress your emotions

All of these things create perfection

At least, on the outside.

No One

Who the hell is perfect?
Certainly not me.
I cry
I break
I scream

Who the hell is perfect?
Certainly not me.
I trip
I stumble
I fall

Who the hell is perfect?
Certainly not me.
I have opinions
I have thoughts
I have emotions

Who the hell is perfect?
Certainly not you.
You yell
You accuse
You berate

Who the hell is perfect?

No one. That's who.

So why do you expect of me
What I can't expect of you?

Snow

Snow

Dreary
Cold
Wet
Slipping cars
Sliding feet

Rushing Past
Blinding the world
Frantic
Howling
Terrifying

Snow

White
Soft
Powder
Sledding children
Shaping snowmen

Slowly drifting

Blanketing the world
Calm
Silent
Peaceful

I was Fine

Life
has its ups
Downs
All arounds.

Everything
Seemed in order.
School
Homework
Friends.

I thought
I was fine.

I wasn't.

I didn't know
I had half a soul.

I didn't know
I was alone.

I didn't know
something was missing

Until I had you.

Love Languages

I don't know if you know this.
But,
I love you
Has many different forms.

Be safe.

I miss you.

I wish you were here.

<3

You're my home.

Darling.

Sweetheart.

Love.

Dear.

Sleepyhead.

I don't know if you know this.
But,
I love you. Be safe. <3
Is really
I love you. I love you. I love you.

Monsters

The world is full of monsters
Who prey on those who can't see them
Invisible but to a special few

They like to hide in your hair
And cling to those unaware
Who's unending cry is "life's not fair!"

The world is full of monsters.
I just thought you should know.
The world is full of monsters.
Cut them off and let them go

Do you know what I am?

Do you know what I am?

I am the knife in your gut:
Stabbing
Twisting
Destroying

I am the animal in your waist:
Biting
Pressing
Gnawing

I am the ocean from above:
Squeezing
Suffocating
Encompassing

I am the current of emotion:
Changing
Slithering
Flowing

I am the life in your veins:
Dripping
Staining
Leaving

Do you know what I am?

Unexpected

Floating softly through the air without a sound
Slowly falling towards the ground
Fluffy, soft, and white piles abound
Children laughing and kicking it around
Until….

"That pile is up to your knees!
You know you have allergies!
Get out of those cottonwood seeds!"

Ships

I was sailing alone
Adrift in the world.
Battling monsters
Is scary when
No one has your back.
Sailing through a storm
Is harder when
No one is there to keep you afloat.

Then you appeared.

Friendly Face

Struggling to get up this day,
You find your world colored in gray.
You don't know why or how
But you have to   push   forward
And find your strength somehow

Step (exhausted)
   By
      Step (can't do this)
         By
            Step (messed it up again!)

You make it outside.
And squint?

A small blob of color
Bounding down the path

   Closer
  And
  Closer
 And
Closer

Scrabbling.

Panting.
Desperate
To see you.

The small ball of color
Wriggling in your arms
Jumping on your chest
Unknowingly spreading
Love
And
Color

Faster and faster it goes
From your head to your toes

And when you look around you see
That gray is not how the world
Is meant to be.

Finally!

Yay!
Your wedding day is finally here!
Amid tremendous amounts of fear!
Delays and
Masks and
Capacity limits
It wasn't so bad to wait an extra year
In order to celebrate with those who are dear.

Help Me

Can't breathe
Can't focus
Can't think

Help me

It hurts
It stings
It chokes

Help me

Drowning
Trembling
Harming

Help me

Hands sweating
Heart racing
Mind panicking

Help me

I'm here

I'm here

Arms holding
Hands pressing
Fingers rubbing

I'm here

Loving
Comforting
Grounding

I'm here

It's okay
It's okay
It's okay

I'm here

Focus on my voice
Focus on my hands
Focus on my breaths

I'm here

Beach Walk

Waves crashing against the land,
Sun shining on the sand.
Took a walk up a dune,
Quickly turned into a running buffoon.
Every step lands in fire,
The situation turning dire.
Bound into the dune grass for salvation,
Only to find further damnation.
Each small blade felt like a knife,
As we ran for our life.
Down to the water we flew,
A cool, refreshing, inviting blue.
As we hit it with a splash,
We knew our ordeal was over at last.

Are we There Yet?

This drive is long.
And boring.

Farm
Farm
Farm

Farm
Farm
Farm

Hey a horse! Hi!

Tree
Tree
Tree

Tree
Tree
Tree

Are we there yet?

Car
Car

Car

Car
Car
Car

I need a nap.

Zzz
Zzz
Zzz

Zzz
Zzz
Zzz

Hey. Wake up.
We're there.

Engagement

I love you today, and will tomorrow.
Especially in torment and sorrow.

Your soft shy smile illuminates the room.
Extinguishing any lingering gloom.

The joy is like the summer sun's warm kiss.
Sudden laughter brings bright bubbling bliss.

I will love you forever if you'll let-
Joining hands walking into the sunset.

Summer Bonfire

Cricket chirps fill the air
The fire crackles without a care
Leaves fill the sky high up above
Sharing it all with the ones you love

A Visit

What day is it today?

It's Monday Grandma
Do you know who I am?

You're….hmmm….Sam?
What day is it today?

It's Monday Grandma
I finished college

Oh that's wonderful!
What day is it today?

It's Monday Grandma
I bought a car

Ooooo. What color?
What day is it today?

It's a deep, dark purple
It's Monday Grandma

When is dinner?
What day is it today?

It's soon. Do you want me to take you?
It's Monday Grandma

Yes. I think I'd like that.
What day is it today?

It's Monday Grandma
I say and I know
The next time I visit
The knowledge of today
Will be like summer snow

Loss

He died this morning.
A release from
Indignity
And infirmity.

I know he hated it
At the care home
The people, food,
And space.

Then why am I left
With a gaping hole,
Broken,
And sobbing?

I visit her,
So she's
Not alone
And grieving.

"She doesn't remember."
I talk to her
Pretending
To be fine.

A marriage of 56 years
A beautiful life together
And I believe
She forgot to be sad.

Working from Home

I paused for a moment
My concentration truly spent.

Standing up to take a break
An opportunity is yours to take.

Darting around my stretching body
Ignoring that I'm feeling shoddy.

I turn to find my chair
Became something to share.

Sleeping soundly is my cat
Right where I literally just sat.

Moving Out

They don't want me to move out
All they do is scream and shout.

They plot behind my back
Deliberating the perfect attack.

They say I'm leaving all I've known
That I will be out there all alone.

They second guess every choice
Drowning out MY voice.

They completely ignore what I say
Hoping that it will make me stay.

They make me struggle from the start
Not seeing how it tears me apart.